All Gone Strange

David Mosey

William Cornelius Harris Publishing

In collaboration

With

London Poetry Books

ISBN 978-1-911232-53-7

William Young

34 Birchwood Close, Bordesley Road SM4 5NH
London Poetry Books

Contents

3

Introduction

I worked for many years as a part-time electrician and ward orderly at a rural psychiatric hospital before I trained as a lawyer. Some of these poems, lyrics and pictures are stories from my youth that were inspired by those hospital jobs and by my brief career on a river steamer, my love of homemade go-karts, the interplanetary illusions of my friend Roger and the challenges encountered at village discos ('Borocourt', 'Captain Pedro', 'Is it a goer?', 'Roger said his dad was an astronaut' and 'Saturday night').

Some items relate to distressing current events ('All gone strange', 'Aye Aye here comes the A I', 'Bloody Unicorns' and 'Ice ice maybe') and others travel back to more cheerful, chaotic times in a rundown London flat with no heating at all and some artistic Finns next door ('Belt buckle blues', 'Diane was a theatre usherette', 'Filming in the park', 'Hello Cécile', 'Helsinki bath-time blues' and 'My dustman's an old man').

Several pieces celebrate the foibles of my beloved parents who were greatly affected by World War Two, who remained inseparable and who died elegantly within four days of each other in 2012 ('My dad came from the docks', 'Good morning', 'Mum shares a room with Rose' and 'Vauxhall Victor').

'The ballad of Gabriel Alix' is taken from my dear Cécile's tiny Burgundian village, where on my first visit I spotted a man at work in his garden who was wearing a transparent waste-paper bin with holes drilled in the front. I said to Cécile's mother: 'Madame, il y a un homme là bas with a bin on his head', and she replied: 'Ah oui, c'est Gabriel Alix. C'est un poète.'

A remarkable number of my songs and poems relate to dancing ('Dancing like dads do', 'Granny's on fire', 'Hippo in a ballroom', 'Jive' and 'Old square dancers'). The others seem to revolve around love, resilience and eccentricity.

Together these stories and pictures offer a brief paddle through the shallows of my soul. I hope you will enjoy the people you meet there.

Some of the songs can be found on YouTube, including an animation of 'Ice ice maybe' kindly created by Alex Mosey and Andrew McKenzie. 'Ice ice maybe' is also the title of a fundraiser album that I made for the charity SANE.

I am very grateful to everyone who allows me to perform in public, and in particular to Glenn Bassett, Karl Bevis, George Chopping, Katy Connell, Diego Brown and the Good Fairy, Malcolm Doherty, John Hegley, Doreen Hinchliffe, Laura Kirby, King's College London, Lola Lewis, Nathan Loughran, Debbie McNamara, the Specs (Ian Graham, Charles Morrish, Mark Oglesby), Steve Tasane, Sara Valaguzza, Isabel White and Jason Why.

'No-one said you must be good as gold
It's what you haven't done
That matters when you're old.'

Ian Dury

All gone strange

It's all gone strange
Now extremes ride the range
Where did all these people come from?
Just how the hell
Do they think they can tell
Us where on this delicate earth we belong?

Hoisting their sails
On a ship made of Daily Mails
It's hard to excuse all those views
I try to think well of them
But what the hell again
Don't judge a man by his shoes
But by how he chooses his news

Facing the strange
With a strong urge to rearrange
The dubious flags now unfurled
Try to explain
That we're on the wrong train
A dangerous game in a vainglorious world

Hoisting their sails
On a search for the Holy Grail
It's more a crusade than a cruise
Their need to compel and then
The self-righteous smell of them
Means walking a mile in their shoes
Won't help me to shake off these blues

Aye Aye here comes the A I

There's so much to think about
Too much data too much doubt
There's no time to work it out
So let's not even try

Modern life is not a breeze
Scary news from overseas
Augmented reality's
A future you can buy

So kiss your synapses goodbye
Aye Aye here comes the A I

In the city's burned-out husk
New perfumes appear at dusk
That's the smell of Elon Musk
He's such a fragrant guy

Cyborgs and predictive text
Guarantee effective sex
Grandma says whatever next
Will pigs learn how to fly?

So lift up your eyes to the sky
Aye Aye here comes the A I

Grandma says the Starlink train
Works with Russia and Ukraine
Turns things on and off again
Manipulates the war

Grandma says she's not too old
To compute what we've been sold
It may look big and very bold
But it's bad news for the poor

The small fish are those who will fry
Aye Aye here comes the A I

Every woman every man
Can be Amazonian
If they drive a Bezos van
Until the day they die

Though this work will make us tired
Pretty soon we'll all be fired
When the workforce is rewired
The robots will say hi

They're harmless, no word of a lie
Just hand the controls to A I

Aye Aye Aye Aye Aye Aye Aye
Aye Aye here comes the A I

The ballad of Gabriel Alix

A poem can your life enhance
So come with me and take a chance
But I should warn you in advance
We're going abroad, we're going to France
Yeah France, pack socks and pants
We're going to France

A village poet once lived there
Un éccentrique whose life we'll share
A man called Gabriel Alix
And it's through poetry he speaks
But also French, yeah it's a wrench
He speaks in French

He lost his house, it sounds bizarre
He swapped his maison for a car
'Good grief!' you say or 'Ooh la la!'
But real poets go that far
How far is that? Half-way to town
The car broke down

Still Gabriel had liberté
Egalité, fraternité
Being words that he used all the time
Because he'd noticed that they rhyme
Yeah rhyme, it's not a crime
But it takes time

And in his jardin every day
At one with nature in his way

Digging up his pommes de terre
A perspex helmet he would wear
Through which he speaks, Monsieur Alix
While planting leaks

The shape of a waste-paper bin
Une grande poubelle his head was in
Not to look chic or debonair
To filter germs out of the air
Oh yeah, there's germs out there
You should take care

And yet one day a germ got through
It killed him but he says to you
In poetry from over there
Live une vie extraordinaire!
Oh yeah, it's not so rare
If you just dare

Being in a movie

My grotty flat was not a squat
It cost me rent though I did not
Have comfort or amenity
But I did have a Finnish bloke next door to me

The Finn next door was at art school
He said it would be rather cool
To do some filming in the park
And I thought, why not, that's how I'll make my mark

Being in a movie
What could be more groovy?
Being in a movie
That's a cool place to be

But we weren't cool so much as cold
Just hanging round and being told
To sit on tree stumps getting numb
The price of art it seems is a chilly bum

I never did see the result
It's possible that it's a cult
Sensation for Helsinki folk
Filmed in the park by the next-door Finnish bloke

Belt buckle blues

I was late for work, I was on the Northern Line
I was half awake and it was half past nine
I'd forgot my tie with no time to go back
But then I thought that the belt on my old mac
Might do instead but didn't realise
That belts are shorter when compared to ties

My belt was canvass and quite thick and green
But who said ties should not be gabardine?
I also thought it would be quite astute
To tuck my big belt buckle in my suit
Whatever else you may have thought or felt
A tie is longer than a raincoat belt

I got to work and went to see my boss
He looked at me at something of a loss
Unknown to me my buckle had popped out
From in my waistcoat and it swung about
And all my boss could do was sit and stare
At my belt buckle dangling in the air

Now I don't know but I have been assured
The pen is somehow mightier than the sword
And I'm told that many a mickle makes a muckle
But be careful if you make one with a buckle
They say it's quality that counts, not size
But not when you are wearing belts as ties

Bloke with a spear

You say you operate
On the need to know
You tell me when to come and
Say when I should go
How did we get this far
With nothing to show?
If I call you to account you
Give me every blow

You stir up troubled water and
Wobble my canoe
Where I come from that's not
A nice thing to do
Can I explain to you the
Virtue of reward?
You listen carefully but
Then you just get bored

I'm just a walk-on extra who
Stands there with a spear
And if you change the plot you
Make me disappear
So don't tell me it's only
Commitment that you fear
If you're so overcome then
Just come over here

Bloody unicorns

Watch out that unicorn
Is just a horse
Its stupid glued-on horn
Is clearly false
Creatures of bluff and spin
Define the mess we're in
Vendors of unicorns
Show no remorse

A teletubby dawn
For all to see
Political soft porn
On our TV
In fur coats with no pants
Beguiling sycophants
Those bloody unicorns
Are running free

It's all a pantomime
With darker roots
Grabbing what's yours and mine
To fill their boots
Political farces
Heads up arses
In their unicorn suits

Watch out those unicorns
Aren't what they seem
Their strange and ugly forms
Will make you scream

Built in a scary lab
They're out for smash and grab
Those bloody unicorns
Will haunt your dreams

Borocourt

At the Borocourt institution
All the occupants' stories were stored
In mistakes, mishaps and confusion
When the wiring came loose on the ward

I was one of the electricians
A foolish and dangerous novice
I managed to get this position
Through my mum's job up in the office

I knew old George Parrish and Rodney Street
Who walked round the grounds in all weathers
The medical staff had admitted defeat
And left them to wander forever

Rodney packed condoms and similar stuff
In the hospital factory
George stayed with us until he'd drunk enough
Cups of strong and sugary tea

George always mumbled, I struggled to catch
What it was that he tried to reveal
When Rodney and I had a wrestling match
He just crushed me with muscles of steel

Our friendship was an unusual sort
I sat and awaited each docket
They'd both made their home there at Borocourt
And I screwed each bulb in its socket

The Bournemouth identity

Nigel spent the night out in a beach hut
Even though he knew it was against the rules
Nigel shut the door and turned the light out but
Those beach hut inspectors are nobody's fools

They've got the time to play a waiting game
They know the beach hut problem is always the same
How long can an occupant suspend disbelief
As to the need to go outside for personal relief?

It's cosy in the confines of a beach hut
And when he'd checked the cupboard and the folding table
Nigel knew his way round with his eyes shut
So lay down on the floor to see if he was able

Not to have to bend his knees or bang his head
And maybe find the space to fit in his camp bed
The practical companion of an orderly man
When pondering an overnight seaside plan

So don't get in a rut
Go and rent out a beach hut
They're down the prom from the pitch and putt
You'll be cheered up by their colourful variety
Join the forward-looking beach hut society

You wouldn't say that Nigel was beach nut
He'd never learned to surf or done his life-guard training
The principal attraction of a beach hut
Was where to watch the waves from if it started raining

But then if you are sleeping inside
When an inspector calls there's nowhere to hide
And Nigel in his hut received a bad shock
When his inspector fastened up the outside padlock

It turned into a long night in the beach hut
Woken up by seagulls walking on the roof
By morning Nigel knew each plank and each strut
Of beach hut woodwork when he was let out as proof

That seaside visitors who are inclined to messing
With proper hours of beach hut use should learn a lesson
But Nigel learned that night he'd found a home a
Single chap could occupy as a beachcomber

So have you got the guts
To get down among those beach huts?
Do it now, I don't want no ifs and buts
When it's rainy by the sea the wet stay in their rooms but
The tough get going to rent a beach hut

Captain Pedro

I worked a Salter's Steamer on the
Reading to Wallingford line
Churning up the water in the
Summer season Thames sunshine
The rule of the river is fairly clear
Aim for the lock and away from the weir
You get that bit right and
Your day should turn out fine

A steamer goes forward
And sometimes in reverse
I learned that much yet the
Sailors they weren't averse
To mocking my lack of nautical skill
They said that I belonged behind a till
So I was the purser and to
Prove it I had a purse

Pedro was our captain's name
A master of the steamer game
I was useless but he
Hired me all the same

A purser does the bookings and
I'm afraid to say
I left a troop of Brownies on the
Thames towpath one day
The Brown Owl's words were more than frank
As we rammed into the riverbank

23

And we loaded on the Brownies like a
Farmer loads bales of hay

Captain Pedro I'll succeed
I've got all I'll ever need
And I love the smell of that
Dark green river weed

I looked on Captain Pedro as though
He was my friend
And in a friendly way he told me
It was the end
Of my river steamer cruise career
He said someone who couldn't steer
Was not the sort of sailor upon
Whom he could depend

Captain Pedro couldn't see
The river was the place for me
He didn't sense our
Close affinity

Dancing like dads do

When you're dancing like dads do
Yeah yeah yeah
You'll be shrugging off all of that
Wear and tear

You can shake your head like you've
Lots of hair
Though it's better if there's no
Mirror in there

You can do a dance a little
Like the twist
Getting down with no reason
To resist

You can make a gesture with a
Rebel fist
Feeling good although you're really
Rather pissed

You're in the groove and you can take
Some risks so
When they play punk you will start
To pogo

There's just no limit to the
Moves you share
When you're dancing like dads do
Yeah yeah yeah

Dermot's thermos

Dermot seemed on top of things, as fit as
an old flea
He didn't have an ailment or a bug or
allergy
Yet he walked around each morning to the doctor's
surgery
With his folded morning paper and a thermos
full of tea
To a waiting room of patients for some human
company

Dermot had a partner once but she'd long since
expired
And he'd lost touch with friends before the time that he
retired
So a thermos full of tea instilled the energy
that fired
His spirits as he ventured out to do what was
required
And sit with pasty faces for the warmth that he
desired

A sturdy thermos plays its part
It keeps a heart of glass well hid
An end to loneliness can start
With two cups in a screw-top lid

Dermot gripped his thermos and he held on
to his pride
When asked by the receptionist if he would

step outside
And he struggled for an answer but he knew
he must decide
If to say he had a broken heart was something
that implied
That his visits to the surgery could still be
justified

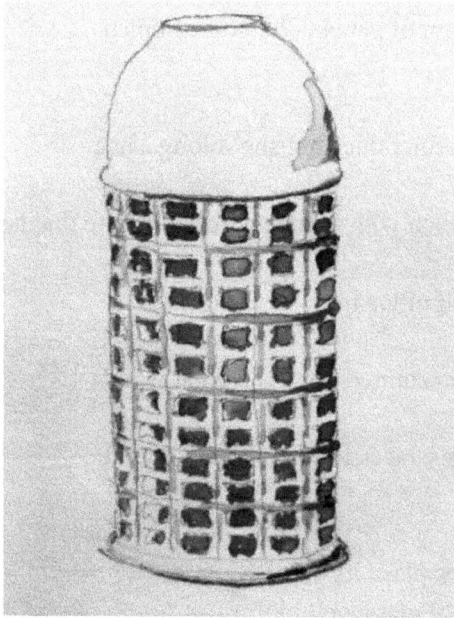

Diane was a theatre usherette

Diane was a theatre usherette
Sensitive and easily upset
In the dark she seemed more self-assured
As she showed you which seat would be yours

That was in the days when we were poor
P.I.L. graffitied on our door
Earning money can be quite a strain
Sitting round is better in the main

Oh Diane
What's your plan?
What's your plan?

Diane and her boss had an affair
Though it's true they made an awkward pair
At the crucial moment to her shame
Found that she was calling his surname

On your own, another one-night stand
Fish need bikes like you needed a man
Keep your spirits up as best you can
Breakfast kippers in the frying pan

Oh Diane
Toast and jam
Toast and jam

Good morning

My dad like all true gentlemen
Would courteously try to reach
Out to the hearts of strangers when
He said good morning on the beach

For dad's wartime generation
Duties should not be evaded
Such as cheerful conversation
While resisting being invaded

And so I try to emulate
My father's forthright, friendly ways
Good morning I say - though I hate
Those strangers who avert their gaze

Granny's on fire

Granny just won't act her age
Going to gigs lets granny rage
Against the dying of the light
She's an awesome sight

Gran won't take her zimmer- frame out
For a gentle stroll
You can't put her inner flame out
She's got rock and roll

Granny's been clocking
Up the miles it's shocking
But a surgical stocking
Doesn't stop her rocking - Granny's on fire!

Grandma's got no time to fit in
Lumbago or cramps
What's the point of sitting knitting?
She's standing next to the amps

Grandma's footsteps lead her to
The Forum, Kentish Town
What on earth is Grandma up to?
She's up to getting on down

Dressing audaciously
Ageing ungraciously
Dancing quite spaciously
Grooving voraciously- Granny's on fire!

Hello Cécile

Hello Cécile
Here's how I feel
I think that after all these years
We might have something real
I hope that you
Might feel the same
Though demonstrative
Is not your middle name

We made our marriage promises
In Finsbury Town Hall
Our party was chaotic, there
Were people wall to wall
The fancy white lace dress worn
By your older sister
Beguiled a younger guest who
Asked if he could kiss her

For the lovers from our past and
All the chips that we cashed in
My auntie gave us a pedal bin
To quench a thirst for solitude
We didn't ought to dwell on
Our neighbours gave us a watermelon

For the things that might get fractured
In life's fragile lottery
A potter made us some pottery
For the mixture of emotions
Caused by all that we have seen

My uncle gave us a soup tureen

Hello Cécile
Excuse my zeal
I savour every moment like
I savour every meal
The laughs I have with you
They move me to the core
And you know that laughter
Shows what love is for

Helsinki bath-time blues

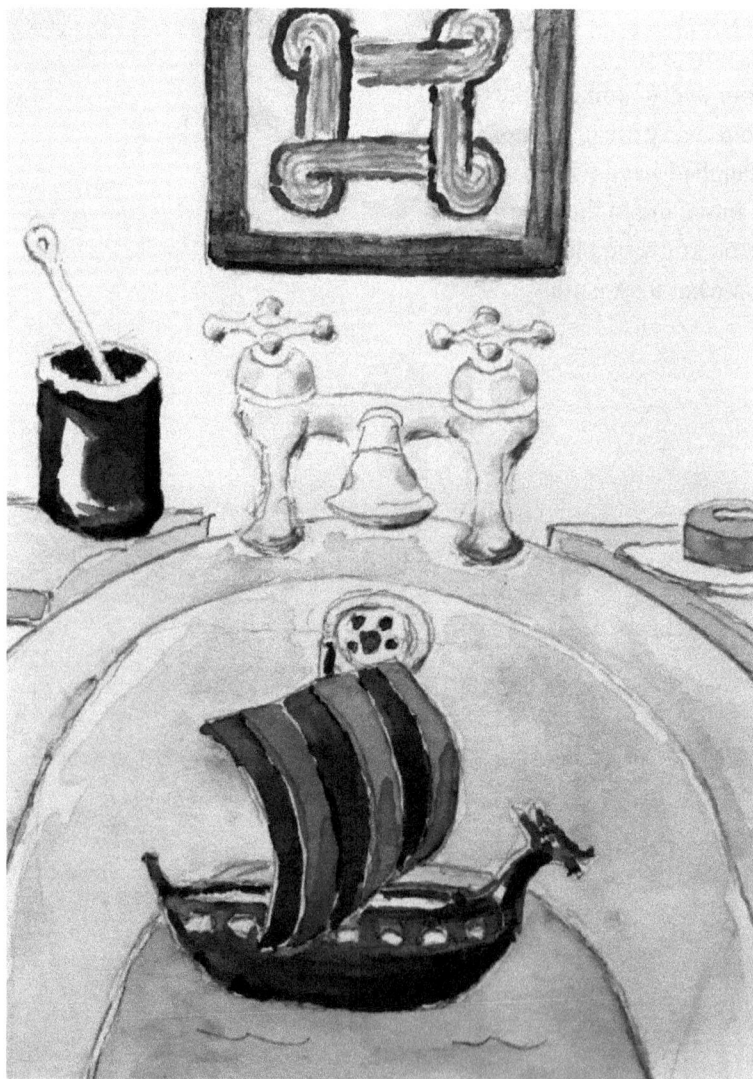

I went for a bath at the home of my
Finnish neighbour
I had no hot water he was doing
Me a favour
He said get in, cleanse your skin of all
That is grotty
I said thanks a lot, no-one likes
To be spotty

And fifteen minutes later I was dressed and I was dry
But the Finn just stood there and asked me why
He was aghast, he said not so fast
Where I come from we like to make a hot bath last

So get in, get in said the Finn
Where I come from a short bath is a sin
You call that a bath?
You're having a laugh
Where I come from the minimum's an hour and a half

So I had a second bath just to
Do what was right
And I lay there in the water as the
Day turned to night
The Finn said a soaking does us a
Power of good
And a Finn pines for his bath more than a Norwegian would

He said when you're stressed, a hot bath is best
You take off your reindeer hat and your vest

Your sealskin boots and those layers of wool
By which time the bathtub should be quite full

He told me in Finland bath-time can be
Quite cathartic
On account of it being so chilly up
Near the Arctic
He showed me his bathtub toys like his little Viking boat
And a long-haired Finnish troll doll
Made of rubber that could float

And I, I wish I could swim
Like troll Finns, troll doll Finns can swim
And some Finn would keep us together
We'd float in the bathtub for ever and ever

But I said no, I said no to the Finn
I don't need a bath, I've already been
In fact I've been twice
And though it was nice
My wrinkled skin is testament that I have paid the price

Hippo in a ballroom

I'm dancing like a hippo in a ballroom
I'm dancing like a rhino in a china shop
I'm dancing like a bison in a small room
I'm dancing for my life as though I'm never going to stop

I'm dancing like I'm standing on my shoelace
I'm dancing like I've got a pebble in my sock
I'm whirling like a dervish with a blue face
I'm dancing for my life as though I'm never going to stop

Oh, won't you dance with me?
I'm old but I've got both my knees
Oh, won't you dance with me?
And we'll dance for our lives as though we're never going to stop

I'm dancing like a dingbat at a disco
I'm lurching like a llama doing the lindy hop
I think of all the dances I will miss so
I'm dancing for my life as though I'm never going to stop

Ice ice maybe

An iceberg coming up the Thames won't
Make a change
A melting mountain shows that we can't
Rearrange
The chairs on the deck of our own Titanic
Perfecting our tans when we ought to panic
And the beasts on the iceberg find that
Kind of strange

On the iceberg the walruses
Will grunt
They say the time has come to be
More blunt
We should turn the heat on demented deniers
Who will see us all sizzling in deep-fat fryers
'Cos the glacial pace of change is just
A stunt

But innit awful when the Innuit cannot roam?
And ain't it pesky if an Eskimo has no home?
Their ice maps are illegible
Their snow's no longer sledgeable
And all their trusty huskies see
Is water where the ice needs to be

On the iceberg a row of
Baby seals
Watch it melt and explain what
This reveals
The way we're going we'll soon be rubbing

The ice caps out which is just like clubbing
The world to death and a seal knows
How that feels

Yet global warming really could be so much fun
If we find ourselves a tasty place in the sun
Where we can all sit back, relax
With trotters up and on our backs
Just dozing while the ice floe cracks
With no need to face up to facts

Til we're face to face
With the baleful stares
Of fractious, anxious
Angry, hungry
Bloody great big bi-polar bears

Those bears will eat you up and they
Won't leave crumbs
Then they'll need a place to park their
Arctic bums
They'll come to your kitchen and try to squeeze their
Great big bear chests into your big chest freezer
To prepare for when the real
Heat-wave comes

I'm waiting for you

And most of all I find
I haven't got a clue
If I know anything
I owe it all to you
I was a stranger in
A dark and foggy land
So I reached for your hand

I'm not sure why you
Make me wait so long
I feel weak when I
Know I should be strong
I'm alright even
Though you prove me wrong
While I'm waiting for you

There are so many things
That I don't understand
What is the modern way
To be a decent man?
It's not so easy to
Stay cheerful through the night
While I wait for your light

Is my liberty a
Blessing or curse?
Have the gears of love been
Thrown into reverse?
I've a feeling this could
Go from bad to worse

While I'm waiting for you

Can it be that good things
Come to those who wait?
While I'm waiting I have
Got to get things straight
If I live in hope or
If I die in vain
All the rest stays the same

I'm not sure why you
Make me wait at all
I suspect that you're
Never going to call
Will you crush my hopes or
Gently let them fall
While I'm waiting for you?

Is it a goer?

What ancient skills can we impart
To stimulate a youthful heart?
Some garage bench technology
That kids can touch and smell and see

Let's build a wooden go-kart so
We pass on something that we know
To show the old are not so daft
And that we understand a craft

Those pushchair wheels will spin around
Above the flashing stony ground
Our kids will gasp in fear and hope
Outdoors, alive and on a slope

They'll love the planks, the screwed-on strut
The string to do the steering, but
They'll learn the crucial thing that makes
A go-kart go is there's no brakes

Jive

Life just rushes on
Here's a question, let me ask it
Where's my mojo gone?
Look in that wastepaper basket
Down at The Palais
I can find my lost libido
I've just got to say
There are times I really need to
 Jive

As we start to rust
And the chrome comes off our bumpers
We just can't be fussed
To take off our woolly jumpers
Don't feel put upon
There are places we can nearly
Fly, just get out on
Some old dance floor where we really
Jive

Who was it who thought
We should show restraint or caution?
Life is much too short
Full of darkness and extortion
Things could be much worse
When I'm holding you I come to
Life, I'm not averse
Under this electric sun to
Jive

Just too straight

A cop pulled me over to the side of the road
She said where d'you get that hat?
It's got to be a breach of the Highway Code
To drive in something like that

I said I work hard to look this cool
Would you like to have a drink with me?
She said here's a ticket you silly old fool
For it's plain for all to see

That you're just too straight
Yes, you're just too straight
I'd let you off with a caution mate
But, hey, you're just too straight

I like to go to the bad side of town
Pretend I'm a reprobate
You've got to get up if you want to get down
But I don't stay up too late

A crazy dude in a shady bar
Said what can I deal you this time?
I said I'm ready to go quite far
So make mine a lager and lime

'Cos I'm just too straight
Yes I'm just too straight
I want to jump but I hesitate
'Cos, hey, I'm just too straight

When you are straight you walk the line
And never make a fuss

47

The middle of the road is fine
Til you're hit by a bus

If I've become too straight
For sex 'n' drugs 'n' rock 'n' roll
I need to contemplate
The inner workings of my soul

I will travel with the mystics
Learn to fast and meditate
Though without my tea and biscuits
I just hyperventilate

'Cos I'm just too straight
Yes I'm just too straight
I'd like to learn to levitate
But, hey, I'm just too straight

Ken loves lovat

Ken loves lovat, how Ken must love it
On the sturdy clothes Ken must covet
Like corduroy for the smell of it
Or moleskin for the hell of it
A colour that's not brown or green
Lovat is more sómewhere in-between

Lovat's known to be quite practical
Outdoors it is more than tactical
It's weatherproof and logical
It looks so ecological
Disguising every awkward stain
Also turning darker in the rain

Ken's old trousers are a lovat must
They're the mainstays of his woodland trust
For striding out through wastelands
In elasticated waistbands
And how they make him feel tonight
Reminds Ken of his lovat first sight

Kettle in the bedroom

It's tough on the road, it can get you down
A dreary hotel in another town
So the hardcore rockers all need their pot
In which to brew some tea and keep it hot

Bands who are touring should at least assume
They'll find a kettle in their hotel room
And after his brew a rock god walks tall
To the bathroom at the end of the hall

While every hotel chambermaid
Will aim to please
A choccie on the pillow-case
Is just a tease
Compared to private tea-preparing
Facilities

In my hotel room just the other day
There was no kettle and I have to say
I hated the view 'cos all I could see
Was an absence where the kettle should be

Rock bands in the genre of heavy metal
Know the value of a well-made kettle
And in their hotel room AC/DC
Provided their own electricity

Now I've no time for showiness
Or luxury
What could a jacuzzi or a hot-

Tub do for me
Compared to instant access to a
Nice cup of tea?

And I don't mind a frilly nylon
Counterpane
And there's a guilty pleasure that
I can't explain
As I slip free digestives from
Their cellophane

So none of us need to get all steamed up
Salvation's waiting in a china cup
At your five- star hotel or B and B
Find the kettle and make a cup of tea

Lockdown

There's not a lot to do in lockdown
But don't you tell me I'm a loafer
I located that lost sock down
The back of my living room sofa
In lockdown

Living life in isolation
Have you got what it takes?
It's a simple calculation
What it takes is a lot of cakes
In lockdown

Birds and badgers and squirrels and foxes
Party for all that they're worth
While we're stuck in little boxes
Wild creatures reclaim the earth
In lockdown

Who'd have thought to walk the line meant
Join a queue and keep your distance?
Jailhouse rock in close confinement
Was the symbol of our resistance
In lockdown

Mum shares a room with Rose

Mum shares a room with Rose
What secrets could that pair disclose
Of living through the Blitz?
Mum's home and work took direct hits
A dig for victory
Her Jack shot down in Germany
And yet the struggle to survive
Made mum feel never so alive

Mum and Rose are in a care home
They both know that it's not their home
But it will do
In their day to have it hard meant
Suffering intense bombardment
During World War Two

Rose shares a room with mum
Sometimes they're chipper, sometimes glum
Just sitting up in bed
Mum's half asleep but in her head
She can locate the keys
To unlock war-time memories
And Rose will cry if someone croons
Those 1940's dancing tunes

Rose still craves the cakes and sweeties
That bring on her diabetes
She wants some fun
And mum finds it most provoking

That she had to give up smoking
Aged eighty-one

Rose and mum in their room
Where who would I be to assume
That they don't share a laugh
Each cosy in her curtained half
To travel back in time
The last but one stop on the line
Until the lights of youthful zest
Are blacked out for eternal rest

My dad came from the docks

My dad came from the docks
He wore suspenders with his socks
Because that was the norm
When he came out of uniform

The army said look smart
My dad's a man who put his heart
And all his demob pay
Into a bookshop in Thorpe Bay

Posh blokes and newspaper vendors
Thanked the Lord the day he sent us
Peace in Europe and a trend as
Sturdy as their sock suspenders

Dad's shop was bound to fail
'Cos naughty books were not for sale
Beneath my dad's counter
A soldier's honour that was down to

My dad aged eighty-nine
Wore sock suspenders bought online
But when all's said and done
He fought the war and the war won

Always be kind to the nation's defenders
Though their stories drive you round the bend as
They've never had as dependable friend as
My dad's extendable sock suspenders

My dustman's an old man

My local dustman's an old man
He empties bins the best he can
One thing about his job he loves
Is wearing great big rubber gloves
They are his armour but he can't abide
It if some sticky substance slips inside

My dustman's got a dodgy heart
He rides up front in the dustcart
His mates all say hey come off it Stan
Ride on the back like a real dustman
In the open air that is the way to live
As a council waste disposal operative

Stan's the man who takes out my bin
His life is virtuous, free from sin
Stan's the man who takes out my bin
Takes it out but he's not taken in

Although my dustman's an old man
Life won't run through his hands like sand-
wiches left crumbling in a bin
He keeps his mind sharp as a pin
When asked Stan what is it like growing old?
He says better than dying, I've been told
Stan pauses and then he adds deadpan
In the end though we're all just dust - man!

Old square dancers

Old square dancers don't lose their style
They're cowboys at heart all the while
But down at the hoedown
As they start to slow down
Their moves are more dosey-docile

Pandora the randy panda

Pandora the randy panda planned
A panda family
Her partner said hang on a mo'
It's also up to me
This tango needs both hers and hims
And I'll not pander to your whims

Pandora's partner's keeper said
Between us, man to panda
Although it's right in principle
For you to take a stand, a
Need for newborn life old mate
Means you will have to demonstrate

Some love for your Pandora
So your union can bear fruit
Now show how you adore her
And don't leave until you shoot

Pauline

(with apologies to Dolly Parton)

Pauline, Pauline, Pauline, Pauline
I'm begging of you please don't take my van
Pauline, Pauline, Pauline, Pauline
Please don't take it just because you can

You don't know what it meant to me
When you asked to be lent the key
You said it was to check on the spare tyre
But that was just a cunning plan
To drive away and leave your man
I can't believe that you'd be such a liar

Although it is a rusty heap
I love my van and I can't keep
From crying thinking of you at the wheel
Although it gives a bumpy ride
We used take it side by side
Now you're off on your own think how I feel

I need my van to do my work
It isn't mine it's just a perk
So I can get round my deliveries
It isn't right it isn't fair
I miss my van it isn't there
Without my van all life is vanity

Pompeii poetry

A poet recorded the way
Vesuvius came to Pompeii
When coated with lava
He noted he'd rather
Have gone out of town for the day

Roger said his dad was an astronaut

Roger said his dad was an astronaut
Stuck his neck out but never thought
We would check
He told us they kept a rocket at home
We said let's see it and went round
To inspect
The interplanetary size
Of Roger's load of porky pies

Roger's dad had flown a fighter jet
He had a classic car at home yet
It was not
The same as him going to outer space
So Roger lied all the way to his place
What a clot
Reality was not enough
So Roger made up cosmic stuff

Oh Roger
You were such an artless dodger
Always had a rather loose
Relationship with the truth

Our comic book claimed that it could make
Spaceships appear but to give kids fake
Hope is bad
They sold a magnet with magic powers
By rotating it for hours and hours
You'd been had
But Roger stared hard at the ground
And waved his magnet round and round

Roger got a job in a Reading boutique
And he turned all his tales into sales technique
He did fine
Then he tried the motor trade
Got caught cheating, I'm afraid
He did time
The men who deal in motorcars
Have got no time for life on Mars

And Roger's dreams of outer space
Just disappeared without a trace

God knows what you were all about
But hey there Roger over and out

Sad dog on a string

You lead me up and down
Like a sad dog on a string
Sad to see I'm easily led
Again
I trot behind you
Just a sorry sort of thing
Hoping for attention now
And then

You keep me in a box
Like a bird with a broken wing
Nursing my ego when
You can
I make my bed among
The breadcrumbs that you bring
Not knowing what you want
Or when

You are taking such a liberty
Observing how far I
Might bend
I can't say I mind captivity
I have no honour to
Defend

Saturday night

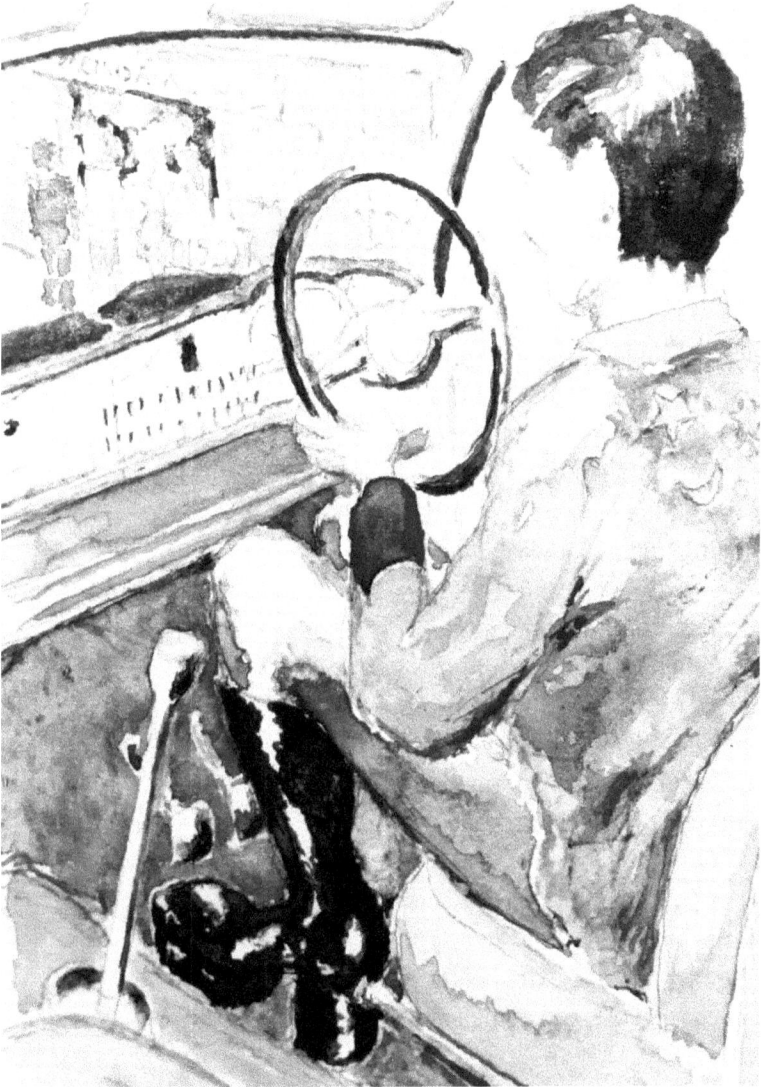

Disco light refraction
On the sparkles of a party dress
Mirrors her reaction
When a fight breaks out she's unimpressed

Where is the attraction
Of a bloke with blood all down his shirt?
Romance loses traction
When her boyfriend behaves like a berk

Dreaming of a miracle
With all the older girls at school
When a tie-dye t-shirt showed
The world that you were really cool

Walking on the wild side
Of the little town that we came from
Dancing to T Rex in
Ways that mostly did not get it on

We all know a teenage dance floor
Can be quite a rowdy place
Ziggy makeup means you run the
Risk of being punched in the face

Platform boots are awkward when you're
Wearing them to drive a car
But they provide the extra height
You need to get served at the bar

Trenchcoat

Hair of the dog, deep in the fog
Dockside and biding his time
Lost in the dark, lighter won't spark
Blindsided walking the line

Profile is low, nowhere to go
Ready to give up the fight
Once in a while he just has to smile
At the things that he sees in the night

Taken to task, emptied his flask
Trenchcoat has had his last snort
Time running out, losing his clout
Life can be brutish and short

Time rolling by, fear in his eye
If there's a case he ain't on it
Here comes the man, slaughterhouse van
Shining a beam on the bonnet

Over the hill, run of the mill
It had to come sooner or later
Leave it to me, nothing to see
I'll send him to meet his creator

Vauxhall Victor

An oil-stained concrete garage floor
Showed what Vic's Saturdays were for
Since cars will not maintain themselves
Vic kept well-stocked garage shelves

Motorcar care means sacrifice
No time to spare, Vic's only vice
Sat on his workbench made of steel
Used for straightening out a wonky seal

Short and stocky, not so large
Were Victor and his old garage
Both built in brick before the war
They don't make garages like that no more

Vic's Vauxhall had a classic look
He kept his vehicle by the book
Not for him go-faster stripes
Or twin exhausts or extra lights

And Vic always had good manners
Throughout his mortal span
And his garage had good spanners
For spanners maketh man

No wheel came off with Vic in charge
Of wheel nuts in his old garage
For Vic life could not get much better
When flushing through his carburettor

An old garage can feel like home
When you are polishing your chrome
Though Victor's Vauxhall wouldn't win a race
Each hubcap showed his smiling face

And when Vic left his garage a
Particular delight
Was to think of his recharger
Recharging his car battery overnight

Short and stocky, not so large
Were Victor and his old garage
Both built in brick before the war
Except of course the up and over door

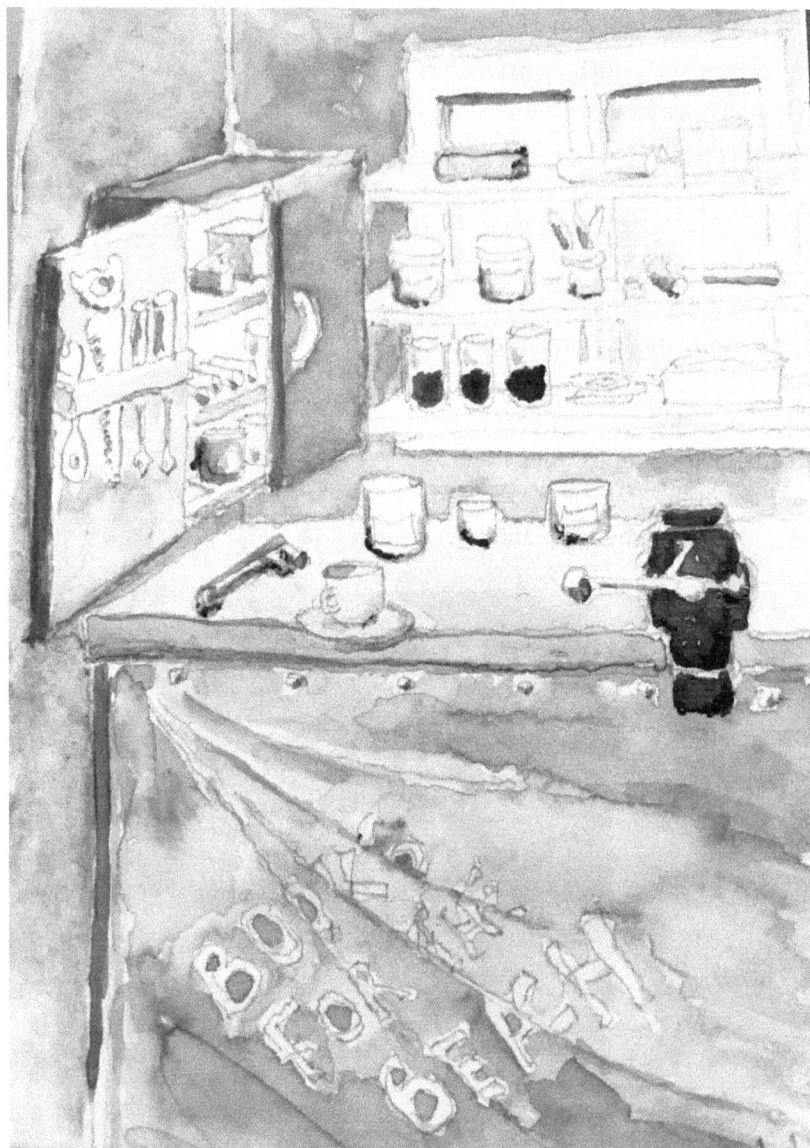